Corporate Acquisitions and Mergers in Latvia

Corporate Acquisitions and Mergers in Latvia

Valters Kronbergs

This book was originally published as a chapter in Corporate Acquisitions and Mergers.

General Editor: Peter Begg

Wolters Kluwer

Published by:
Kluwer Law International B.V.
PO Box 316
2400 AH Alphen aan den Rijn
The Netherlands
E-mail: lrs-sales@wolterskluwer.com
Website: www.wolterskluwer.com/en/solutions/kluwerlawinternational

Sold and distributed by:
Wolters Kluwer Legal & Regulatory U.S.
920 Links Avenue
Landisville, PA 17538
United States of America
E-mail: customer.service@wolterskluwer.com

ISBN 978-94-035-3536-4

e-Book: ISBN 978-94-035-4026-9
web-PDF: ISBN 978-94-035-4036-8

Contents

Kronbergs Čukste

Kronbergs Čukste Levin is a full-service Latvia-based law firm. With its cooperation partners in the Baltic States and elsewhere in Europe, it can provide not only full pan-Baltic legal services but also European Union (EU)-wide legal solutions.

The law firm is known for its industry focus in a number of service lines: Corporate Commercial M&A, FinTech, Banking and Finance, Data Protection, Energy and Utilities, Real Estate, IT/IP and Litigation. Our main principle of service is international quality with local expertise.

Author

Valters Kronbergs is the managing partner and co-founder of Kronbergs Čukste Levin. He has been a member of the Latvian Bar for over twenty years. He is also a member of the Law Society of Ontario. Valters has acted for multinational and domestic companies, government agencies and banks on transactions since 1993. He is also a practising arbitrator in commercial disputes.

Kronbergs Čukste Levin

Muitas iela 1, Riga, Latvia

Tel.: 371 29208166

Fax: +371 67043804

1 LOCAL ECONOMIC, POLITICAL AND CULTURAL ASPECTS

[01] Latvia is a country in the Baltic region of Northern Europe. It is bordered to the north by Estonia, to the south by Lithuania, to the east by Russia and to the southeast by Belarus and by a maritime border to the west with Sweden. According to the Central Statistics Bureau of Latvia, it had a population of 1 876 000 as of early 2022. Its national currency is the euro. The capital of Latvia is Riga.

[02] Latvian is the official language. The most widely used minority language is Russian, the native language of about 25% of the population. English is widely used in business and tourism.

1.1 Labour Costs

[03] In the first quarter of 2022, the average labour cost was EUR1 297 *gross* per month, and this has been steadily growing since 2008, at least partly due to increasing minimum wages and changes in labour taxation by the government of Latvia. The COVID-19 pandemic deteriorated the overall number of employees in Latvia; e.g., in 2021, the deterioration of employees in comparison with 2020 was 3.2%. However, at the beginning of 2022, it registered an overall deterioration in the unemployment level with a simultaneous increase in vacancies. Labour market trends in 2022 show that the number of vacancies is increasing in comparison to the last year, and unemployment is decreasing, in particular for skilled workers. Demand for unskilled labour, based on the latest reports, is increasing.

During the first quarter of 2022, the unemployment level in Latvia was 6.7%, but in the capital city Riga, it was 6.5%.

1.2 Natural Resources and Infrastructure

[04] The country has a temperate seasonal climate. Most of Latvia is comprised of fertile lowland plains and moderate hills with vast forests alternating with fields, farmsteads, and pastures. Latvia has hundreds of kilometres of undeveloped seashore lined by pine forests, dunes, and continuous white sand beaches. Latvia has the fourth-highest proportion of land covered by forests in the European Union (EU), after Finland, Sweden, and Slovenia. Forests account for 3 497 000 ha (8 640 000 acres) or 56% of the total land area.

[05] The Latvian road network is well developed, with ongoing upgrades in progress.

[06] Latvia's railroad is part of the rail network accessing places as far as the Russian Far East. Transshipment of goods occurs primarily by either rail links or shipping lanes. However, since the phase of the Ukraine conflict starting 24 February

2022, due to the EU and other international sanctions, railroad cooperation with Russia has deteriorated.

Riga, Ventspils and Liepāja are the three main ports of Latvia. Seven smaller ports include Salacgriva, Lielupe, Engure, Mersrags, Roja, Kolka and Pavilosta. Most transit traffic uses the top three ports, and half the cargo consists of coal and oil products. In recent years, the Rail Baltica project, intended to connect Baltic rail networks with those of Western Europe, has been moving forward; with the design stage now finished and the construction phase ongoing, the completion of this project is scheduled for 2026. The Riga Freeport is also experiencing several development projects aimed at enhancing its capacity. For example, the Kundzinsala development project is being carried out in three stages for completion by 2025, with total investments being hundreds of millions of euros.

[07] Riga International Airport remains the busiest airport in the Baltic States, providing flights to over seventy destinations.

1.3 Political System

[08] Latvia has a stable parliamentary democracy led by the prime minister and a cabinet of ministers. The Republic has a president, whose role is largely ceremonial, except for specific limited powers such as putting up candidates for prime minister and approving legislation. Latvia is a member of the Organisation for Economic Co-operation and Development (OECD), the United Nations, the EU, the Council of Europe, the North Atlantic Treaty Organization, the Organization for Security and Co-operation in Europe, the International Monetary Fund, the World Trade Organization, the Council of the Baltic Sea States and the Nordic Investment Bank. Latvia has been a member of the OECD since 2016. This process has seen many improvements in the Latvian legal system and in its business and investment environment as Latvia implemented OECD recommendations.

[09] Latvia is well integrated into the global financial system. Latvia is ranked nineteenth in the world by the Ease of Doing Business Index 2020 prepared by the World Bank.

1.4 Legal System

[10] The civil law-based Latvian legal system is grounded in the principles laid out in the Constitution of the Republic of Latvia and safeguarded by the Constitutional Court of the Republic of Latvia. EU legislation has also been an integral part of the Latvian legal system since 1 May 2004. The legal system of Latvia belongs to the family of continental civil law legal systems with noted similarities to the German legal system, from which Latvia borrowed many legislative solutions following the restoration of independence, with the French legal system being another major influence.

[11] While arbitration is sometimes selected as the form of dispute resolution, most parties look to the Latvia court system to resolve disputes. In recent years, Latvia has seen a reduction of time in the period between the commencement of proceedings and the issue of court judgments.

[12] In 2021, Economic Affairs Court was founded, and it has jurisdiction over business-related matters, such as shareholder disputes, competition infringement cases, construction disputes, insolvency cases of credit institutions (banks), investment disputes, and breaches of AML regulations. During its first year, the Economic Affairs Court has had 241 court cases, 51 of which are civil cases (mainly corporate and shareholder disputes), 45 criminal cases and 145 proceedings in relation to breach of AML regulations.

In 2022, the reform of court system was also finalized, and its goal was to maximize efficiency of the Latvian judicial system. As a result of the reform, there is only one court of first instance in Riga having jurisdiction over all administrative territory of Riga City and Riga District.

[13] During the COVID-19 pandemic, in order to ensure control over the spread COVID-19 virus, Latvian public bodies issued a number of different legal regulations in order to maintain functionality during the pandemic. Although most of these regulations were targeted at eliminating the spread of COVID-19 and the majority of the restrictions have been cancelled, some of the newly introduced rules have remained in place as they proved to be convenient also for post-pandemic life. One such example is remote participation and voting in the shareholder meetings, which was originally introduced to enable shareholders to participate in corporate meetings during the overall prohibition on assembly. Now the Latvian Commercial Law grants a shareholder the right to cast a vote even before the meeting is assembled, provided that the documents submitted by the shareholder allow for identifying the particular shareholder and the vote is received at least one day before the scheduled shareholder meeting. In other cases, remote shareholder meetings can be assembled on the board's initiative or on demand of shareholders holding at least 20% of shares.

As of 24 February 2022, the Latvian government implemented EU and other international sanctions against Russia. Since Latvia is an EU Member State, all sanctions adopted by the EU Commission and Parliament are in force in Latvia. Hence, all restrictive measures provided by the EU sanctions prohibit numerous activities in the business area, and others (such as finance, trade of fossil fuel and transportation) are restricted or completely prohibited.

1.5 Current Economic Aspects

1.5.1 Economic Growth

[14] According to the Latvian Central Statistical Bureau, in 2022, economic growth continued, with gross domestic product increasing by 6.7%, compared to 2021.

[15] The unemployment level in Latvia has slowly reduced in the last nine years. In 2018, it was 7.6%, but in 2022, it was down to 6.5%.

1.5.2 M&A Trends

[16] The growth in environmental, social and governance-conscious investment has manifested itself in a number of private equity M&A transactions across the Baltic region in 2021. Such considerations were present in one of the largest pan-Baltic 2021 undisclosed M&A transactions, with an estimated value of EUR1 bn, for the sale of an 80% capital stake in the largest European producer of sustainable wood pellets, Graanul Invest AS, in the third quarter of 2021.

The acquisition of one of the largest pharmaceutical-holding companies in the Baltic region, Olainfarm AS, was concluded at the end of 2021 with acquisition by AB City AS of a 69.15% capital stake for a total amount exceeding EUR90 m via buyout and delisting.

A majority of the recent M&A transactions have been performed primarily with small- and medium-sized enterprises (SMEs), which were targeted by Nordic and Baltic companies to facilitate regional expansion through consolidation of capable local competitors.

1.6 Main Industries

[17] The key industries of Latvia are forestry, transportation and logistics, warehousing, manufacturing, IT, hospitality, construction, and real estate. In general, there are no restrictions against foreign ownership. However, there are some restrictions on farmland acquisition and the acquisition of land adjoining waterways. Moreover, since restrictive measures were implemented by EU authorities, ownership by Russian or Belarusian persons or entities is restricted.

[18] Private equity is mostly local and active in sourcing investment opportunities. Venture capital is mostly seen in the context of seed capital. Strategic corporate buyers have been active in the banking and energy sectors and notably in the fuel and retail sector.

1.7 Cultural Aspects

[19] Latvia is open and welcoming to foreign investment. It has a number of industrial parks specializing in western standards of service, warehouses, communication technologies, ports, railways, and the largest airport in the Baltic countries.

[20] There are no restrictions regarding the citizenship of company owners. However, *Commercial Law* requires disclosure of the ultimate beneficial owners of all companies registered in the Latvian commercial register. Due to the sanctions and other restrictive measures against Russian and Belarusian entities and nationals, the changes in the shareholding and ultimate beneficial ownership will not be registered where an entity or nation that has been included in the sanction persons' list appears in the ownership or control chain of the Latvian company.

[21] The procedure for company registration is straightforward and relatively inexpensive. Minimum share capital requirements generally provide for an investment of at least EUR2 800 with an option to pay EUR1 400 upon registration and the balance of EUR1 400 within one year of registration of limited liability companies (SIAs). Joint-stock companies (AS) have a minimum share capital of EUR35 000 at the present time (until it is phased out in the near future).

[22] There are strict legal restrictions against giving gifts to government officials. Moderately valued gifts between private sector business partners are not uncommon.

2 THE REGULATORY FRAMEWORK

2.1 Business Vehicles

[23] The most common forms of business vehicles used in Latvia are:

- SIA (limited liability company).
- Sole proprietorship.
- Partnership (general partnership and limited partnership).
- AS (joint-stock company).

[24] The most common form of corporate vehicle used is the SIA. Preconditions to registration include:

- execution of documents of incorporation (the memorandum of association, the articles of association and the register of shareholders being the most substantial), the signatures of the founders' representative on the registration form, board members' signatures on consents to be elected and board members' signatures on the register of shareholders;
- selection of board (and if applicable supervisory council and auditor);
- presenting information about the ultimate beneficial owners of the new entity (which should be updated or re-confirmed each time when the members of the board of directors are changed or there are changes in the shareholding of the company);
- payment of share capital (at least EUR2 800 for a full-size SIA) into a designated bank account within the jurisdiction;
- payment of state fee to the Register of Enterprises (ranging from EUR75 up to EUR225 depending on the number of founders);
- submission of an application to the Register of Enterprises.

[25] After the end of the accounting year, the board of directors must execute the annual accounts of the company and submit them to the auditor (if the company size threshold is exceeded which triggers the audit requirement). After receipt of the auditor's opinion (and, if the company has a council, also after the council's report has been received), the board of directors must call a meeting of the shareholders at which the shareholders are to approve the accounts. The annual accounts of the company (and the sworn auditor's report if such exists) must be submitted to the State Revenue Service within a month of approval of the annual accounts and not later than four months (seven months for medium and large companies) after the end of the accounting year under the *Annual Report and Consolidated Annual Report Law of Latvia*. The State Revenue Service thereafter must send a copy of the annual accounts to the Register of Enterprises that, in turn, provides public access to the documents received.

[26] The company has an ongoing duty to notify the Register of Enterprises of any changes to share capital amounts. Share capital may be increased or decreased (but not below EUR2 800 for an SIA and EUR35 000 for an AS) but only on the basis of a decision of a meeting of the shareholders. A decision on changes to share capital may be taken if not less than two-thirds of the votes of the shareholders present so vote unless a higher threshold for voting is set out in the articles of association. If a decision on changes in share capital is reached, then amendments must be made to the articles of association as regards the share capital. Both the decision and the amended articles must be notarized.

[27] Changes to the board of directors must be reported to the Register of Enterprises of Latvia. Members of the board of directors may be elected and recalled only by a decision of the meeting of shareholders. Members of the board of directors may also resign from the office at their own initiative by delivering a written notice to the company.

[28] Generally, the minimum amount of share capital of an SIA is EUR2 800.

[29] The typical management structure of an SIA consists of the following:

- the meeting of shareholders – the decision-making body of the company and the highest authority in the company;
- the board of directors (management board) – the executive body of the company carrying out the business operations of the company;
- the supervisory council (if such has been formed) – the supervisory body of the company, charged with protecting shareholders' interests between meetings of the shareholders and supervising the work of the board of directors.

[30] A meeting of the shareholders has jurisdiction to take decisions on any such issues as are within the competence of the board of directors or the council. In such cases, the shareholders who voted for the relevant decision are liable for any losses incurred as a result of such decision. In addition, there are certain issues that are only within the competence of a shareholders' meeting.

These are:

(1) amendments to the articles of association;
(2) increase or decrease of share capital;
(3) election or recall of members of the supervisory council;
(4) election or recall of members of the management board;
(5) approval of the annual accounts and the distribution of profits;

(6) election and recall of the auditor, company controller and liquidator;
(7) bringing of actions against members of the board of directors, council members, founders or shareholders;
(8) termination, continuation, suspension, renewal or reorganization of the activities of the company, as well as the entry into, amendment or termination of an intra-group of companies' agreement;
(9) other issues which, in accordance with the law or the articles of association, are within the jurisdiction of the shareholders.

[31] The board of directors may consist of one or more members who are primarily tasked with representing the company, and they can do so solely or jointly, depending upon the model of representation set out in the articles of association. Its duties also include:

- providing information to a meeting of shareholders as regards transactions concluded between the company and shareholders, members of the council or members of the board of directors;
- maintaining proper records of the shareholders of the company and the ultimate beneficial owners of the company, timely reporting of the changes in this information to the commercial register maintained by the Register of Enterprises corresponds to the actual facts;
- convening the regular shareholder meetings for approval of annual financial statements as well as convening extraordinary shareholder meetings at the request of the shareholders;
- at least once every quarter, submitting to the council (or to the shareholders) a report on the activities and financial state of the company, as well as to notify the council (or the shareholders) without delay as regards deterioration of the financial state of the company or other significant circumstances relating to the company's commercial activities.

[32] If the company has established a supervisory council, the articles of association may provide that the chair of the board of directors is appointed by the council. Otherwise, the chair is selected by the board of directors.

[33] Remuneration for members of the board is set by a decision of the supervisory council, but if the company has no supervisory council, then by a shareholders' resolution. The Commercial Law of Latvia sets out that the remuneration has to be consistent with the board member's duties and the financial well-being of the company but does not place limits on its size, leaving that to the discretion of the shareholders' meeting.

[34] If a supervisory council exists under the articles of association of the company, its role is as follows:

(1) to elect and recall members of the board and to supervise the activities of the board;
(2) to monitor that the business of the company is being conducted in accordance with the law, the articles of association and the decisions of the meeting of shareholders;

(3) to examine the annual accounts of the company and to consider recommendations by the board for allocation of profits and to draw up a report;
(4) to represent the company in court in actions (if any) brought by the company against members of the board, and actions brought by the board against the company, and to represent the company in other legal relations with members of the board;
(5) to approve transactions or consent to transactions between the company and members of the board or supervisory council, related parties or the auditor;
(6) to examine in advance all issues which are within the competence of the meeting of shareholders or which, pursuant to the proposal of members of the board or the council, have been proposed for discussion at the meeting of the shareholders and to provide an opinion on such issues;
(7) to give consent for a decision of the board to increase the company's share capital and to approve amendments to the articles of association of the company if the meeting of shareholders has authorized the board and the council to increase the share capital within set limits without a repeated meeting of shareholders.

[35] Where applicable, the meeting of shareholders elects a sworn auditor whose duties are to audit the annual accounts of the company and to submit an opinion thereon. An auditor may not be a shareholder, a member of the board or supervisory council member of the company itself, or a person interested in the commercial activity of the company. If the company is part of a group of companies, the auditor is not permitted to be a member of the board or supervisory council of a dependent company or dominant undertaking.

[36] An auditor is professionally liable to the company and third parties for losses attributable to the errors or omissions of the auditor. An auditor is not liable for any losses caused as a result of violations committed by the governing bodies of a company, except in cases where the auditor knew or ought to have known about such violations but failed to refer to them in its opinion, in which case he is liable along with the members of the corresponding governing body.

[37] Ordinarily, executive authority is exercised by the members of the board. All members of the board have representation rights which may be exercised solely or jointly. There is no specific document that must be used where executive authority is being exercised by the members of the board.

[38] Unless and to the extent that the articles of association specify otherwise, members of the board represent the company jointly.

2.2 Laws Affecting M&A

[39] The main laws involved in M&A activity in Latvia are the following:

- Commercial Law.

- Competition Law.
- Credit Institutions Law.
- Group of Companies Law.
- Financial Instruments Market Law.
- Share Buy-back Law.
- Civil Law.

[40] The *Credit Institutions Law* includes specific provisions regarding the reorganization of credit institutions (banks), and the *Share Buy-back Law* governs share buyout procedures of listed companies.

2.2.1 Mergers

[41] Under a merger, one or several companies (the acquired companies) transfers all of its/their property to another company (the acquiring company), whether already existing or established as a result of such merger. The acquired companies cease to exist without liquidation procedures, and all the rights and obligations of the acquired companies are transferred to the acquiring company. The shareholders or members of the acquired companies become, respectively, shareholders or members of the acquiring company. The process becomes effective once the respective entries with the commercial register are made. Official notifications to creditors are required by law. In some instances, the creditors of the companies involved in such processes are entitled to request security for their respective claims.

2.2.2 Demergers

[42] Under a demerger, the demerging company transfers all or part of its assets into one or more acquiring companies and either continues its operation or ceases to exist without undergoing liquidation procedures. The respective rights and obligations related to the assets transferred under the demerger agreement are transferred to the acquiring company in accordance with the terms of the demerger agreement. Shareholders of the demerging company or the demerging company itself may become a shareholder in the acquiring company. The process becomes effective upon the respective entries with the commercial register being made. Official notifications to creditors are required by law. In some instances, the creditors of the companies involved in such processes are entitled to request security for their respective claims.

[43] A transformation is a restructuring process as a result of which one type of company, for instance, an SIA, is transformed into another type of company.

[44] Under a business transfer, all or part of the assets and liabilities of a company (defined in Commercial law as an 'undertaking') can be transferred to another entity by entry into a sale (transfer) of business agreement. Unlike the mergers and demergers described above, the business transfer is not subject to any specific procedures or registrations that have to be followed in order to become effective. Specific rules apply with respect to joint liability of the transferor and acquirer of the business for the liabilities established prior to the date of transfer of business; these are aimed at protection of the creditors, and the parties to the transaction cannot rule out the rights of creditors to seek satisfaction of their claims from either of the two parties to the business transfer transaction.

[45] In addition to the above basic transaction types regulated in the *Commercial Law*, specific rules as to publicly listed AS provided for in the *Financial Instruments Market Law* and *Share Buy-back Law* must be followed if a certain amount of stock is acquired (i.e., mandatory and voluntary stock redemption).

2.3 Relevant Regulatory Authorities

[46] Since most of the changes in the company's structure and corporate documents are subject to filing or registration with the public register, either in order to become effective or to ensure that they are made known to the public, the main governmental authority involved in the M&A process is the Register of Enterprises. It deals with formal compliance of the documents, whereas other government authorities evaluate the contemplated transaction on a substantive level.

[47] The Competition Council is a regulatory body whose task is to ensure a properly functioning competitive environment in the market. The most significant functions of the Competition Council include assessment of the effects of intended mergers as well as prevention of abuse of dominant position or the conclusion of anticompetitive agreements. A merger notification must be submitted to the Competition Council for approval in relation to mergers of companies having an annual turnover of EUR30 m or more in total, provided that there is no merger participant having an annual turnover of less than EUR1.5 m. A failure to obtain prior approval of a merger from the Competition Council where so required may trigger a fine of up to 3% of the acquirer's net turnover in the last financial year.

[48] The Financial Capital Market Commission is responsible for controlling financial and capital markets and their participants by monitoring compliance with applicable laws, regulations and commission decisions. Not all companies have to secure their approval for an M&A transaction – the Financial Capital Market Commission deals with companies whose shares are included in regulated markets, and the acquisition of whose shares brings a duty to notify the Commission of the transaction and increase of shareholding in a listed company. Acquiring certain percentages of shares can come with an obligation to issue mandatory share buyback offers if the target company shares are included in a regulated market. It must be noted that the Financial Capital Market Commission is to be merged with the Bank of Latvia as of 1 January 2023, and all functions and prerogatives which are carried out by the Financial Capital Market Commission will be performed by the Bank of Latvia.

[49] As regards annual accounts and tax issues, the State Revenue Service is the main regulatory authority concerned with tax compliance.

[50] It takes between one and three business days to incorporate a company or review any documents subject to registration with the Register of Enterprises. While it is not mandatory for communications with applicable institutions to be made through advisers, such communications might be advisable in cases involving complex issues, such as obtaining a merger permit from the Competition Council, especially if language barriers between the parties to the transaction and the responsible authorities are a concern. The Financial Capital Market Commission is also very forthcoming in discussing the application of law to specific matters.

2.4 Controls/Restrictions on Foreign Investment

[51] Since 24 February 2022, EU institutions have issued restrictive measures targeting Russian and Belarusian authorities and all individuals and entities which are aiding the Russian government in waging war in Ukraine or connected with them. Latvian government did not issue any national sanctions, but there are restrictive measures applied in Latvia which are based on EU regulations and other international sanctions regimes.

2.4.1 Specifically Regulated Area: Real Estate

[52] There are special requirements regarding the acquisition of land by foreign purchasers. While citizens and companies of the EU can acquire land under the same conditions as nationals, foreign investors from outside the EU may not acquire land located:

- in the border zone of the state,
- in protected nature areas in zones of nature reserves,
- in the protection zone of coastal dunes of the Baltic Sea and the Gulf of Riga,
- in general, land within the protected zone of public reservoirs and waterways,
- agricultural and forest land in conformity with the territorial planning of local government (it should be noted that as of 2014, Latvian law provides special rules concerning agricultural land – the restrictions are aimed at ensuring that agricultural land is, in fact, used for agriculture, possibly making it a less lucrative investment target in some cases), and
- land containing mineral deposits of national significance.

[53] In order to acquire land, a foreign investor who is either a natural person or a legal entity from outside the EU is required to submit an application to the applicable municipal council. The municipal council will thereafter make a determination as to whether the acquisition of the land is in compliance with restrictions set out in normative regulations and planning documents. Special restrictions apply to agricultural land; namely, the law grants a right of first refusal to the State Land Fund to purchase agricultural land. On the other side, there are income tax exemptions for the seller in case the agricultural land is sold to the State Land Fund.

[54] There are no specific restrictions on foreign directors or managers. A local partner is not required, and the presence of a governmental official is not necessary

(although in 2014, there was a failed law reform initiative requiring at least one management board member to be a Latvian citizen, a Latvian non-citizen, a citizen of EU, European Economic Area (EEA), or a Swiss citizen.) As a practical consideration, it is often thought useful to have a local director, particularly for communications with Latvian government institutions. No special requirements exist as regards permits to trade.

2.5 Incentives for Foreign Investment

[55] Since 1 July 2010, the Latvian government introduced amendments to its *Immigration Law* in order to encourage investments in real estate. Under this, a foreigner may request a temporary residence permit for a period not exceeding five years if it makes certain investments, such as:

(1) paying EUR10 000 into the state budget and making investments in the share capital of a company from EUR50 000 to EUR100 000 depending on the number of employees in the company, yearly turnover and yearly tax payments (for smaller companies, a restriction of no more than three residence permit eligible investors per company applies);
(2) buying a built-up immovable property in Latvia valued at not less than EUR250 000, subject to a number of conditions such as the absence of unsettled tax debts, citizenship of the seller, cadastral value of the property and payment of at least 5% of the property's value into the state budget;
(3) an investment of at least EUR280 000 in a credit institution from Latvia for a term of at least five years and subject to a payment of EUR25 000 into the state budget of Latvia;
(4) purchase of government obligations (with no interest) with a nominal value of at least EUR250 000, subject to a payment of EUR38 000 into the state budget of Latvia.

A foreigner may request a temporary residence permit for a period of time not exceeding three years if the foreigner plans to implement activities in the Republic of Latvia to manage and develop an innovative product, and the following conditions are present:

(1) Within three months after the decision to issue a temporary residence permit, the foreigner must have been registered as a member of the board of directors in a capital company which has been registered in the commercial register for no longer than one year and within the scope of which the foreigner plans to manage and develop an innovative product.
(2) After the temporary residence permit is issued, within twelve months, the foreigner submits information on previous early-stage risk capital investment in the amount of EUR30 000 or information on progress report of the product for the period implemented by the capital company, which

confirms that the capital continues to support the innovative investment during this period in terms of design, manufacture or development.

[56] In addition, if all the necessary conditions are fulfilled, a temporary residence permit may be simultaneously obtained by the family members of the investor.

[57] Government guarantees against expropriation or nationalization are widespread under numerous bilateral and multilateral investment treaties. Although there is an expropriation law in existence, in practice, it is hardly ever used. The government, in practice, treads lightly on property rights.

[58] Foreign lenders may take security over local immovable property. There are no currency controls over the transfer of funds, but funds transferred to offshore jurisdictions are subject to withholding tax. Non-bank consumer credit has also experienced changes as solvency checks are now mandatory, and debtor databases have been introduced to combat loan dependency.

[59] There are no exchange controls or currency regulations affecting foreign investors, but transactions with entities located in low-tax or tax-free jurisdictions are treated less favourably from a corporate income tax (CIT) perspective.

2.5.1 Specific Issues of Company/Securities Law

[60] The *Commercial Law* requires that certain approvals from shareholders be notarized before a notary public or signed by secure digital signatures in an effort to combat fraudulent share transfers. For instance, the title to shares in an SIA must be notarized or digitally signed and registered into the register of shareholders maintained by the board of the company. Similarly, management changes are also subject to notarization or digital signature requirements.

[61] Generally, mergers are subject to the resolution of the shareholders' meeting of the company by a qualified majority of votes (this is subject to exceptions on mergers with subsidiary companies – if a merger is performed with a target which is at least 90% owned by the acquiring company, the merger is approved by the target's management board). Business transfer transactions, as well as the sale or acquisition of shares, are subject to shareholders' resolutions only if so required under the articles of association of the company.

[62] Where a merger or demerger is taking place in the form of a regulated reorganization, it is a mandatory requirement that all the creditors are informed of the reorganization via publication in the *official gazette* 'Latvijas Vēstnesis'. Due to amendments in *Commercial law*, such publication will be published in 'Latvijas Vēstnesis' till 30 June 2023. Afterwards, publications on reorganizations will be available on the Register of Enterprises' official webpage. In certain cases stipulated by law, unsecured creditors and partly secured creditors (in respect of those obligations not covered by the security) are entitled to request that their claims be secured by the companies involved in the merger. In cases where the restructuring takes place in the form of a private business transfer agreement, the only remedy for creditors is the general provision of the *Commercial Law* that all companies involved

in such business transfers are jointly and severally liable for creditors' claims. It should be noted that not all asset sales are business transfers in the sense set out in section 20 of the Commercial Law of Latvia, so it is possible to acquire parts of a business in Latvia without becoming liable to its creditors.

[63] Neither a reorganization (merger/demerger) nor a business transfer transaction can result in termination of the employment contracts of the relevant employees. Employment contracts can only be terminated by way of mutual agreement or on the basis of grounds set out in the *Labour Law*, which restricts the employer's rights to unilaterally terminate employment for cause to specifically enumerated grounds only.

[64] A reorganization agreement is subject to approval in the meeting of shareholders. The board of directors is obliged to keep the shareholders informed in case of any material changes in the company's circumstances during the course of the reorganization.

2.6 Form of Consideration

[65] Share capital must be paid up either in cash in *euros* or via material contributions. Material contributions may not include services or incomplete parts of property.

[66] In most cases, an independent property valuation from a certified appraiser registered by the Register of Enterprises is required in the case of material contributions.

[67] There are no restrictions on the disposal of shares acquired as a result of a property contribution. Special restrictions regarding the disposal of shares may be included in the articles of association. A transaction involving the disposal of shares must be concluded in writing and may be subject to rights of first refusal by other shareholders, if there are any.

2.6.1 Security Interests

[68] There are certain formalities required to effect the transfer of shares, land and certain other assets.

Formalities to Effect the Transfer of Shares

[69] In the case of SIA (and non-listed AS), the transfer of shares becomes effective as of the time of making a corresponding entry into the register of shareholders, which is a mandatory internal document of the company. The register of shareholders is maintained by the board, and the entries in it are made on the basis of an application of both parties involved in the share transfer transaction or a transaction document. Entries must be certified by the signature of the chairperson of the board and by both the seller and the buyer of the shares. The signatures of the named persons must be notarized (or alternatively, digitally signed), and the relevant folio of the register of shareholders must be filed with the Register of Enterprises. As mentioned above, changes in the shareholding trigger an obligation for the legal entity to report changes in the information about its ultimate beneficial owners.

Formalities to Effect the Transfer of Real Estate

[70] In order to give effect to the transfer of land, registration with the Landbook has to be made. Such registration is performed on the basis of a notarized application and upon payment of state fees and duties.

Formalities to Effect the Transfer of Other Assets

[71] Other registers apply to certain other assets, such as the Road Traffic Safety Directorate register for automobiles.

2.6.2 Costs and Fees

[72] Except for the transfer of title to real estate (where a state duty is payable in the amount of 2% of the real estate value), the state fees payable to effect asset transfers are generally modest in size. For example, the state fee for a change of management board and share ownership does not exceed EUR120, and there are no additional fees tied to the value of the transaction or the nominal value of shares being sold. The associated notarization costs depend upon the nature of the notarized document and its volume but are unlikely to exceed EUR100 in total. For example, a certification of authenticity of a signature on a document costs EUR11. As mentioned, notarization costs with respect to corporate changes can be avoided by signing the documents digitally and generally, the digital signatures issued in other EU Member States are accepted in Latvia.

2.6.3 Dividends

[73] Dividends may only be paid on the basis of a decision of the shareholders and out of distributable profits and not otherwise. Yearly and interim dividends are possible. Interim dividends can only be calculated and paid once every three months and out of no more than 85% of the profits earned in the period since the previous payment of dividends. There are no restrictions on a domestic company's ability to distribute dividends, whether to domestic shareholders or foreign shareholders.

[74] The *Commercial Law* requires that dividends may not be determined, calculated and paid out if it is apparent from the annual accounts that the company's equity is less than the total amount of its share capital.

2.6.4 Purchase of Own Shares

[75] It is generally prohibited for a company to acquire its own shares, except under certain limited conditions, for instance, where a shareholder, which is a legal entity, ceases to exist. The company is barred from exercising any rights arising from the relevant shares and must dispose of the shares within a period of one year after such acquisition has taken place. If it is not possible to sell the relevant shares, these have to be eliminated by reducing the company's share capital.

2.6.5 The Corporate Veil

[76] Unless specifically agreed to the contrary with the relevant creditor, parent companies are not liable for the debts or any other liabilities of their subsidiaries in Latvia. In the case of directors, however, they are jointly liable for losses that they have caused to the company except in so far as they can prove they were acting as honest and careful owners of the company. It should be noted that some developments in the Supreme Court of Latvia case law demonstrate that the lifting of the corporate veil could be applied in the future.

2.7 Insolvency

[77] An insolvency administrator may choose to sell a company where the sale of the business is the most beneficial outcome for the creditors or may decide to sell the assets of the company separately. Under the Insolvency Law of Latvia, any proceeds from the sales of individual assets or the sale of the entire business of an insolvent company will first go to the company's creditors and only then to its shareholders, proportionally to their participation.

[78] With respect to liquidation, if a sale is consistent with the plan of liquidation and is at fair market value, there is little risk of the transaction subsequently being unwound by an administrator in insolvency.

2.8 Choice of Law

[79] Choice of law, jurisdiction and arbitration clauses are recognized and enforceable in Latvia. The parties are free to agree on dispute resolution clauses, including dispute resolution procedures before arbitration tribunals.

2.9 Specific Rules on Public Takeovers

[80] The rules on public takeovers are found in the Latvian *Financial Instrument Market Law* and the *Share Buy-out Law* adopted in 2022. The latter was adopted with the purpose of simplifying the buyout procedures, and to some extent, they repeat the regulation of the buyout process initially set out under the *Financial Instrument Market Law*. The competent regulatory authority is the Financial and Capital Market Commission (FCMC). The Commission has jurisdiction to issue regulations binding upon market participants. It also monitors compliance of market participants through the *Financial Instrument Market Law* and *Share Buy-out Law*, as well as FCMC's regulations.

[81] The Latvian Central Depository (LCD) is the sole central securities depository in Latvia and administers the Latvian central register of publicly issued securities. The LCD performs the function of safe-custody of securities, clearing and settlement for securities trading and management of corporate actions, and provides other services related to securities. Banks operating in Latvia also maintain securities accounts for their clients, and the Commercial Law of Latvia provides that shareholders of an AS may request that their shares be moved from the LCD to a securities account in a commercial bank.

[82] The *Share Buy-out Law* provides for the following types of takeovers (being a buyout of shares of a company whose shares are admitted to the regulated market): mandatory, voluntary or a final share buyout offer. The type of offer depends upon the existing structure of the shareholding in the particular company. In particular, if the buyer has reached a certain percentage of participation, this may trigger a right or a duty to make a buyout offer. The *Share Buy-out Law* also provides for the possibility of buyout of the shares in case the shareholder meeting has passed a resolution on exiting the regulated market.

[83] Generally, takeovers can be characterized as contractual offers via an offer document. It is possible that under certain circumstances, there may be several competing buyout offers in relation to the same shares of the company. The law does not provide for court-approved schemes of arrangement.

[84] Takeovers are notified to and monitored by the Commission, and in most cases, the transaction can be completed only upon receipt of the Commission's consent. The *Share Buy-out Law* and the regulations issued by the FCMC and the Depository contain quite detailed provisions on how the respective procedures are to be carried out, including the content of documents, the rights and duties of the parties involved and the procedures and pricing rules for mandatory buyout offers. It is also possible to use the offer approved by supervisory authority in another EU Member State to acquire the shares listed in the Latvian regulated market.

[85] Under the *Financial Instrument Market Law*, the responsibilities of the management (members of the board and supervisory council) of the target company mainly relate to information non-disclosure requirements. They must issue an opinion on the offer, addressing in particular issues of how acceptance of the offer might affect the company, and must comment on the strategic plans of the potential acquirer of shares and the indirect impact of such plans on employment and the planned location of the business. The opinion expressed by the management has to be made available to the employees and published on the home page of the stock exchange. Management is barred from taking actions that might hinder the successful completion of the offer once they become aware of such offer, and such prohibition remains valid until the end of the offer period (usually between thirty and seventy days).

[86] A party may make a voluntary stock buyout offer and set either a minimum or maximum amount of the shares or a specific category of shares that would be acquired as a result of the offer. If no such limits are set, it is considered that the voluntary buyout refers to all shares of the target company. The new *Share Buy-out Law* does not require that the voluntary offer should result in the ownership of at least 10% of the number of shares with voting rights.

[87] There is the concept of a 'mandatory bid' in the Latvian *Share Buy-out Law*. Under the law, a mandatory offer must be made by a party or by an existing shareholder of the target company who directly or indirectly acquires voting shares such that his/her voting rights are equal to or exceed 30% of the total number of voting rights at the respective company.

[88] The *Share Buy-out Law* lists several exceptions when a mandatory bid does not have to be made, e.g., if the shares were acquired through voluntary bidding or there are no changes in the actual person exercising control over the entity holding at least 30% of the voting rights. Banks and investment brokerage companies are released from the mandatory bid obligation provided that the share acquisition has no purpose of participating in the control over the target company and serves merely as a short-term investment. If the person does not make the mandatory bid, he/she is prohibited from disposing of his voting rights at the shareholders' meeting of the company.

[89] The law provides guidelines as to how to calculate the number of shares to be sold to the bidder during a voluntary bid in circumstances where the current shareholders offer fewer shares or a number of shares exceeding the number of shares indicated in the bidder's offer.

[90] The share purchase is supervised by the FCMC, which reviews and approves the bidder's submission, either allowing or prohibiting the issue of the offer. Information about the bids is published in the centralized information system and home page of the stock exchange. Information about issued offers also has to be published in the official gazette, which publishes official notices.

[91] Under the law, there is a notification requirement upon a person regarding the proportion of his/her voting rights when, as a result of an acquisition or disposal of shares, or of an increase or decrease of equity or any other event, it reaches (or is reduced to) the following percentages of the share capital of a listed company: 5%, 10%, 15%, 20%, 25%, 30%, 50% or 75%. If Latvia is the home Member State for an AS, a person must also notify the proportion of the company's voting rights held by it when as a result of an acquisition or disposal of shares, or of an increase or decrease of equity, or any other event, its percentage of voting shares in the company reaches, exceeds (or becomes less than) 90%.

[92] Neither Latvian *Financial Instrument Market Law* nor *Share Buy-out Law* contains any guidelines on the due diligence process to be conducted in the case of public takeovers. As a listed company, the target company is obliged to publicly announce any material events. Such material events include but are not restricted to a change in management, other corporate changes, the appointment of auditors, approval of annual financial statements, the conclusion of substantial agreements with clients or customers, or information on ongoing court proceedings. The potential buyer may obtain a general overview of the affairs of the target company, but certain information would only be revealed during a due diligence process if this is practicable.

[93] Where the company is controlled by one major shareholder, it might be possible to arrange a due diligence exercise for such company prior to the issue of the offer, and the company's management could then be instructed to assist the potential buyer's consultants in the process without revealing the reasons for the review of the company's files.

[94] The law does not contain any rules applicable to situations in which information about the bid is disclosed prior to its approval by the FCMC.

[95] The Latvian law sets out principles regarding the pricing of a bid only in cases of a mandatory buyout offer. The price in such a buyout should be a fair price calculated in accordance with the principles included in the law, and generally, it is tied to the price for which the shares were acquired during the last twelve months preceding the mandatory offer date, namely:

- the price at which the bidder has acquired the target company's shares. If the shares have been acquired at different prices, the buyout price must be the highest price paid for the acquisition of shares within the last twelve months; or
- the weighted average price of a share on the regulated market or in the multilateral trading system where the relevant stock had the highest turnover within the last twelve months. The weighted average price of a share must be calculated for the last twelve months before the conditions arose which required a mandatory bid;
- the value of a share that is calculated on the basis of the value of the equity capital of the company divided by the number of shares of the company.

[96] If the bidder acquires shares of the company within the period when he was under an obligation to make a mandatory offer, the price for which the shares were acquired (if it is higher than the price offered during the mandatory offer), then this higher price replaces the price offered in the mandatory offer documents.

[97] For a period of six months following the expiry of the validity of the offer, the bidder is entitled to acquire shares of the target company at a price higher than the price offered in the mandatory bid only where all persons who have sold their shares to the bidder receive the difference between the current price and the price at which the shares were acquired during the mandatory bid process.

[98] The same buyout terms have to be offered to owners of the same class or category of shares. If the company has different classes or categories of shares, share prices can be different for different classes or categories of shares.

[99] As regards options or convertible securities, the target company is prohibited from issuing new shares or convertible bonds or changing nominal value of the shares or merging or dividing share issues during the term of the offer.

[100] The bidder's submission approved by the supervisory authority must contain information on sources of financing of the bid and how settlement for the shares will take place. The bidder is obliged to provide documents verifying the sufficiency of funds for the purchase of the shares (usually a letter issued by a bank, investment brokerage company or insurance company).

[101] Conditions are allowed only in voluntary bids, i.e., where a bidder offers such bid, it has to indicate the minimum and maximum amount of shares that the bidder is prepared to acquire. It is also possible to state in the offer that the offer will become invalid if the number of shares offered for purchase does not amount to the minimum indicated by the bidder in its offer.

[102] The FCMC has to be notified of a mandatory bid no later than fifteen days after the occurrence of the circumstances requiring submission of the mandatory bid. There are no terms established for the submission of other types of bids. The above deadline also applies to voluntary bids but is counted from the bidder's decision to make a voluntary bid. The duration of the validity of the bid is permitted by law to last from fourteen to a maximum of seventy days from the date of publishing the prospectus of the offer on the website of the regulated market. There are restrictions on paying the target company's dividends and modifying share categories and nominal values of shares in this period.

[103] Under the law, a voluntary offer is regarded as a competing offer if it is issued in respect of shares of a target company while another offer is in effect with regard to the same shares. If the competing offer is expressed, then the term of the initial offer can be prolonged until the end of term of the competing offer.

[104] The law contains clear instructions as to what documents have to be submitted to the shareholders and the supervisory authority, the FCMC. The FCMC has also elaborated its requirements with respect to the form of relevant documents, e.g., notifications on the acquisition of shareholdings, and has issued guidelines to shareholders of public companies and persons interested in issuing voluntary bids. It is quite common to consult the FCMC in case of questions or uncertainties, and the FCMC typically welcomes such questions. Nevertheless, neither bidder nor the target company may be identified during such consultations.

[105] There are no rules about advertising, press interviews and/or PR activity. The law only prescribes rules regarding the mandatory announcement of the bid and publishing of such information in the official information system or on the websites of stock exchanges and of the target company itself.

[106] As a rule, the buyer acquires control once payment for the shares is made without any other obligations or reservations. Acquiring control over the shares does not automatically result in an obligation to change the constitutional documents or to make any other corporate changes in the target company.

[107] There are compulsory purchase procedures as regards the buyout of shares not yet accepted under the offer. Thus a party acquiring at least 90% of the voting shares may demand that other remaining shareholders sell their shares, and if it does so, then the remaining shareholders have a duty to sell. This offer is called a final share buyout offer. The final share buyout offer is subject to approval from the FCMC. The price per share for a final share buyout offer is determined according to the rules similar to those used in the event of a mandatory buyout bid.

[108] There are two types of consequences in the case of a breach of the rules of public takeovers:

(1) The FCMC, as a regulatory authority, is granted the right to apply penalties to a party in breach of the rules (e.g., where a party has not initiated the mandatory buyout procedures or has not made due notifications in case of an increase of shareholding in the company). The amount of the fine for such a breach is established as being up to EUR700 000 (for failure to express the mandatory buyout offer) and up to EUR100 000 (for other types of breaches of regulatory requirements. FCMC also has the discretion to issue a warning or public announcement about the breach without applying any monetary penalties.
(2) Prohibition against a person from using its voting rights arising from the shares owned by such person (whether directly or indirectly). The law provides that a resolution of the shareholders' meeting is invalid if 'prohibited' votes are used to adopt such resolution and cannot be entered in the public registers. The court, when hearing a case for the annulment of a shareholder decision, invites the FCMC to participate in order to give an opinion on the matter of the dispute and to defend the rights of the shareholders.

2.9.1 Other Relevant Law and Due Diligence Issues

[109] *Law on the Prevention of Money Laundering and Terrorism and Proliferation Financing* is the law under which Latvia has implemented EU Directives No. 2005/60/EC, 2006/70/EC, 2009/110/EC, 2011/61/EU, 2015/849/EU, 2017/541/EU, 2018/843/EU and 2019/1153/EU. This law was recently amended to broaden its scope in respect of the prerogative of the Financial Intelligence Service and cooperation between authorities in AML area.

[110] *The Criminal Law* also contains provisions concerned with anti-money laundering and anti-bribery. Conviction of laundering criminal proceeds may result in imprisonment of between three and twelve years. Terrorism financing can result in imprisonment of between eight and twenty years.

[111] There are no specific environmental or product safety laws that should be considered with respect to foreign investors except the general rules established in the *Environmental Protection Law*, *Protection Zone Law* and other environmental regulations. As regards product safety laws, the requirements are established in the *Goods and Services Safety Law of Latvia*, with some categories of goods and services

having further safety requirements set out in Cabinet of Ministers' regulations. *The Consumer Rights Protection Law of Latvia* also contains some more generalized provisions on product safety.

[112] It is relatively easy to register, protect and enforce intellectual property rights (IPR) in Latvia. Latvia is a signatory to the Paris Convention for the Protection of Industrial Property. Relevant law includes *Copyright Law, Patent Law, Law on Designs, Law on Trademarks and Geographical Indications*, and *Plant Varieties Protection Law*, all of which contain specific regulations. As Latvia is a Member State of the EU, the specific regulations introduced to protect IPR within the EU are applicable. One such regulation is the regulation on the customs enforcement of IPR as part of a comprehensive EU-wide strategy concerning IPR. This regulation seeks to ensure that the rights of the parties concerned are respected by customs through a specific mechanism that was introduced within the EU.

[113] Commercial agency relationships are dealt with under *Commercial Law*. A commercial agent, after the termination of a commercial agency contract, may request corresponding compensation from the principal if and insofar as:

(1) the principal, after the cancellation of the commercial agency contract, gains substantial benefits from transactions with new clients which were originally introduced by the commercial agent;
(2) the commercial agent, because of the termination of the commercial agency contract, loses the right to a commission or remuneration, which it would have had in respect of transactions already concluded, or to be concluded in the future, with clients introduced by it if the commercial agency contractual relationship were to have continued;
(3) the payment of compensation, taking into account all the circumstances, must be expected from the principal on the basis of fairness.

[114] The commercial agent has a right to compensation for losses caused by the termination of a commercial agency contract, especially for unearned expenses and investments where the commercial agent has acted on behalf of the principal in fulfilling the commercial agency contract.

[115] The valuation of intangible assets such as goodwill and IPR is a matter of negotiation for the parties to the transaction. Change of control clauses are occasionally used and are enforceable.

2.9.2 The Due Diligence Process

[116] As in most jurisdictions, it is common in Latvia to conduct a due diligence investigation regarding commercial, financial, tax, property, environmental and other issues. Property rights are commonly verified by investigating the information included in the Landbook (real estate register) and data bases available at the State Land Service, as well as territory development plans developed by each local municipality. Environmental audits are, in certain instances, required by law, and it is generally prudent to conduct such audits.

[117] The target's handling of personal data should be checked for compliance against the GDPR and the Latvian *Personal Data Processing Law*, particularly in view of the substantial fines which may be imposed for violation of personal data protection rules. Industry-specific regulation should also be kept in mind, as further certification or regulation may apply, e.g., in the field of consumer credit, banking or medical services.

[118] Due diligence on the reputation of existing as well as prior owners is sometimes helpful in mitigating the risk of failure to disclose material pre-existing agreements or adverse conditions.

[119] On occasion, acquirers do not take enough care in evaluating particular facts or circumstances about their target. A case in point is that of an acquirer of land who only learned after the acquisition that its building plans were at risk due to elevation restrictions on the relevant land as a result of proximity to radar installations.

[120] Contractual representations and warranties are standard features in purchase and sale agreements. Any failure to disclose during the due diligence process should serve as evidentiary support in further litigation to enforce indemnification where it is not forthcoming voluntarily. Acquirers sometimes negotiate retentions pending the achievement or resolution of specific future conditions.

2.9.3 Role of the Courts

[121] Courts are the main dispute resolution mechanisms in Latvia. Arbitration is also frequently used. Depending upon the scale of the acquisition, it may be advisable to opt for foreign arbitration. Frequent choices include Stockholm and London arbitration under International Chamber of Commerce rules.

[122] Contractual provisions such as restrictive covenants, protection of minority shareholder rights and enforcement of warranty or indemnity claims are generally enforceable but time-consuming to pursue through the Latvian courts. Where it is necessary to look to the courts for relief, litigation may take a number of years. The lack of an adequate system of injunctive relief in Latvia also compounds this problem, sometimes allowing the defendant to continue to harm the claimant's interests during the litigation. The Court of Economic Affairs was introduced in March 2021 and is expected to develop more specialized skills in adjudicating commercial disputes.

3 MERGER CONTROLS: ANTITRUST/ COMPETITION ISSUES

3.1 Relevant Legislation and Competent Authorities

[123] The merger control regime is set out under the *Latvian Competition Law*. Besides the *Latvian Competition Law*, which sets out the basic principles of the merger control regime, specific issues related to merger control (such as the content of and procedure for submission of the merger notification) are governed by a number of subsidiary legislative acts under regulations of the Cabinet of Ministers.

[124] The relevant authority entrusted with the functions of merger control is the Latvian Competition Council.

[125] Latvian competition regulation is also substantially impacted by the regulation adopted at the EU level.

[126] For the purposes of application of the Latvian merger control regime, a merger is defined by *Latvian Competition Law* as:

(1) the merging of two or more independent market participants in order to become one market participant (consolidation);
(2) the joining of one market participant to another market participant (acquisition);
(3) a situation where one or more natural persons who already have decisive influence over another market participant or other market participants, or one or more market participants acquire part or all of the fixed assets of another market participant or other market participants or the right to use such, or a direct or indirect decisive influence over another market participant or other market participants;
(4) a situation where two or several natural persons jointly or a single natural person simultaneously acquires all or part of the assets of two or several market participants or obtains the right to use such assets or obtains direct or indirect decisive influence over two or several market participants.

[127] Under the *Latvian Competition Law*, the Competition Council prohibits a merger as a result of which a dominant position is created or strengthened or which may significantly reduce competition in any relevant market.

[128] If the merger in question meets the thresholds established by the European Merger Regulation, a filing must be submitted to the European Commission.

[129] Mergers which must be notified may only be implemented after the Competition Council has approved them. Therefore, in practice, agreements which establish the basis for the merger usually contain a clause stating that the agreement will only become effective after the Competition Council has approved the intended merger.

[130] If a merger must be notified, but the parties to the merger have failed to do so, a penalty in the amount of up to EUR1 400 per day will be imposed by the Competition Council for each day starting from the day when the filing was required to be submitted. A penalty will be imposed even if the merger is subsequently approved.

3.2 Scope of the Controls

[131] A mandatory obligation to notify applies if one of the following conditions exists:

(1) The combined turnover of the parties to the merger was at least EUR30 000 000 in the previous financial year in the territory of Latvia.
(2) At least two merger participants' turnover in the previous financial year in the territory of Latvia was EUR1 500 000.

[132] The Competition Council may request to notify on planned or concluded merger (which was concluded within twelve months) if:

(1) merger is performed between competitors, and the cumulative market share of the parties of the merger exceeds 40% of the relevant market; and
(2) the Competition Council has reasonable grounds for the proposition that the merger can result in a dominant position or strengthen a dominant position of one of the merger participants.

A merger notification does not have to be submitted in the following cases:

(1) Credit institutions or insurance companies acquiring securities on their own behalf or on behalf of other persons who do not use the acquired securities to influence other undertakings on the relevant market.
(2) The Competition Council may extend the referred to time period on the basis of a submission from the relevant credit institution or insurance company if it proves that the relevant investment within one year was not possible.
(3) A liquidator or insolvency administrator acquires a decisive influence in the case of the insolvency or liquidation of a market participant.

[133] It is an obligation of the parties to the merger to assess whether or not they meet the above-listed conditions. Detailed instructions regarding the calculation of the turnover of the parties to the merger are provided by a specific Cabinet of Ministers Regulation. The definition of market share is provided in the *Competition Law* and corresponds to that established by the *acquis communautaire*.

3.3 Process/Mechanics

[134] According to the *Competition Law*, merger notification must be submitted before the merger actually takes place.

[135] Merger notification must be submitted:

(1) in the case of consolidation – by the market participants who are merging;
(2) in the case of acquisition – by the market participant to which another market participant is being joined;
(3) in the case of an acquisition of decisive influence or of the assets or of the right to use the assets – by the market participant or by a physical person who acquires the decisive influence or the assets or the right to use the assets, as the case may be.

[136] The required content of the merger notification is specified by Cabinet of Ministers Regulation No. 800 of 29 September 2008.

[137] Under the law, an assessment of the merger is carried out with the aim of establishing whether, as a result of the merger, a dominant position is created or strengthened or whether competition is diminished in any particular market. In the assessment of the merger, the following aspects may be considered (the list is not exhaustive):

(1) The structure of the relevant market, the competition created by the market participants and the necessity to preserve and develop competition within the Latvian market.
(2) Restrictions on competition which are directly related to the intended merger, including the types and duration of such restrictions.
(3) The economic and financial situation of the market participants, the availability of alternative markets for consumers and suppliers, administrative and other barriers to market entry, characteristics of the supply and demand for the relevant goods, the interests of intermediaries and consumers, technical and economic development, as well as possible obstacles to competition.
(4) The situation of market participants in the international market and the possibility of export of goods and services of the relevant market participants.
(5) Possible economic or social gains for consumers and society.

[138] The Competition Council, by its decision, must prohibit any merger as a result of which a dominant position is created or strengthened or which may significantly reduce competition in any relevant market. The Competition Council is entitled to permit such mergers, applying binding commitments on the parties to the merger, which may prevent negative consequences of the merger.

[139] A decision of the Competition Council may be appealed to court. The Competition Council is required to adopt a decision regarding the merger within a maximum of four months after the merger notification has been submitted to the Competition Council. Normally, however, a decision is adopted within one month.

[140] The above-mentioned deadlines start running only after a complete merger notification has been submitted to the Competition Council.

[141] In order to expedite obtaining of merger approval, it is advisable to engage in communication with the Competition Council before the actual submission of the notification in order to clarify the content of the notification.

[142] The Competition Council is open to communication with the parties to the merger prior to as well as during the assessment of the merger. However, in view of the complex nature of the merger control regime, it is advisable to seek the assistance of legal counsel.

[143] The Competition Council is obliged to prohibit a merger as a result of which a dominant position is created or strengthened, or the competition in any particular market may be diminished.

[144] After a merger notification has been received by the Competition Council, it publishes information about the intended merger on its web page in order to obtain opinions from competitors and other stakeholders about the effects of the merger on competition in the market. Such opinions are considered during the process of assessment of the intended merger.

[145] The *Competition Law* provides that the Competition Council may allow a merger which would otherwise be prohibited if the parties to the merger provide commitments which prevent possible negative consequences of the merger.

[146] *The Competition Law* does not specify the type of commitments which can be accepted by the parties to a merger. However, it is a general understanding that commitments can be both structural and behavioural.

3.3.1 Timing of Approvals in the Context of a Bid for a Publicly Held Company

[147] When bidding for a publicly held company, it must be borne in mind that a merger which has to be notified can only take place after approval of the Competition Council has been received. In practice, the acquirer may acquire a publicly held company, but it will have to suspend its rights deriving from the ownership of the particular company until the decision of the Competition Council is adopted.

3.3.2 Sanctions for Breaching the Merger Control or Other Antitrust Laws

[148] If a notification of a merger has not been submitted in the cases prescribed by the *Competition Law*, the merger is considered to be illegal, which means that if the merger is not eventually approved, it must be reversed.

[149] If a notification of a merger has not been submitted in the cases prescribed by the *Competition Law*, the Competition Council is entitled to take a decision regarding the imposition of a fine of up to EUR1 400 for each day, counting from the day when the notification should have been submitted. The fine will be imposed, even if the merger is approved, once the notification has been submitted.

[150] If a merger has occurred and it does not comply with the decision of the Competition Council, the Competition Council is entitled to take a decision regarding the imposition of a fine of up to 3% of the net turnover in the last financial year.

[151] The imposition of a fine does not release the parties to the merger from their obligation to comply with the provisions of the *Competition Law* and decisions of the Competition Council.

3.3.3 Anticompetitive Restraints

[152] Engaging in an agreement with the vendor whereby the vendor agrees not to compete with the sold business runs a serious risk of being regarded as an anticompetitive agreement within the meaning of the Latvian *Competition Law*. Anticompetitive agreements are illegal.

[153] However, Latvian *Employment Law* provides that an employment agreement may contain a non-compete obligation. If there is a non-compete obligation in the employment agreement and the employee leaves the company, the employer must pay the employee monthly compensation during the period of application of the non-compete obligation. If the employee breaches a non-compete obligation, he/she is no longer entitled to receive compensation.

[154] A non-compete obligation may be applied with regard to employees for a maximum period of two years after the termination of the employment relationship. According to the *Employment Law*, non-compete obligations must not unreasonably restrain the activities of an employee. Therefore there is a risk that a non-compete obligation will not be enforceable with regard to any geographic markets in which the company in question does not actually operate and compete.

[155] If a management team owns the target company, it may be provided in the share purchase agreement that part of the purchase price will only be paid after the management team has stayed with the company for a certain period of time.

3.3.4 Main Constraints Affecting Competitive Behaviour after the Transaction Is Implemented

[156] The competitive behaviour of market participants is regulated by Latvian *Competition Law*, which mainly prohibits the following.

(1) Conclusion of Anticompetitive Agreements

[157] Under the *Competition Law*, agreements between market participants, which have as their object or effect the hindrance, restriction or distortion of competition in the territory of Latvia, are prohibited and void from the moment of being entered into.

[158] The law does not provide an exhaustive list of types of agreements which may be regarded as anticompetitive. Hence the Competition Council and the Court play a significant role in defining anticompetitive agreements.

[159] There are, however, specific rules (block exemptions) for the assessment of vertical agreements and horizontal cooperation agreements.

(2) Abuse of a Dominant Position

[160] According to the *Competition Law*, any market participant who is in a dominant position is prohibited from abusing such dominant position in any manner in the territory of Latvia.

[161] As with the prohibition of anticompetitive agreements, the law does not provide an exhaustive list of activities which are deemed to be an abuse of a dominant position, leaving it for the Competition Council and the Court to define the notion of abuse of a dominant position.

(3) Engaging in Unfair Competitive Conduct

[162] According to the *Competition Law*, actions as a result of which laws or fair commercial practices are violated and which have created or could create a hindrance, restriction or distortion of competition are deemed to be unfair competition. The law does not provide an exhaustive list of activities which may be deemed to constitute unfair competitive conduct.

[163] Unlike the conclusion of anticompetitive agreements and abuse of dominant position, which can be established by either the Competition Council or the Court, engaging in unfair competitive conduct can only be determined by a Court.

[164] Abuse of *Competition Law* may be established by the Competition Council or by the Court. The only exception is engaging in unfair competitive conduct, which may be determined only by the Court.

[165] In practice, abuse of *Competition Law* is usually established by the Competition Council, and the Court only acts as an appeal body. The Competition Council is seen as an effective watchdog for preserving a solid competitive environment in the market.

[166] Issues related to employment relationships are handled by the State Labour Inspection and the Court.

4 TAXATION ASPECTS

4.1 Nature of the Tax Regime

[167] The tax system in Latvia is developing continuously.

[168] The tax rules are not complex; however, the procedures for application of relevant taxes might be complicated and might require specific knowledge.

[169] The correct application of taxes is monitored by the State Revenue Service of the Republic of Latvia. The activities of this authority are directed rather more towards the collection of more taxes (through tax audits) rather than towards assistance of companies and/or explanation of the applicability of taxes during the ordinary course of their business.

4.2 Liability to Tax

[**170**] Taxpayers in Latvia are both Latvian residents and non-residents. For the purpose of the tax laws, a *private individual is considered a resident* if:

(1) the registered place of residence of such person is Latvia; or
(2) such person stays in Latvia for 183 days or longer during any twelve-month period beginning or ending in a tax year; or
(3) such person is a Latvian citizen who is employed in a foreign country by the government of Latvia.

[**171**] A taxpayer *who is not a natural person is generally considered a resident* if he/she is registered (or if it should have been established and registered) in accordance with the laws of Latvia. Subjects who do not fit into the criteria mentioned above are treated as non-residents of Latvia for tax purposes.

[**172**] The general taxation principle applicable in Latvia provides that Latvian residents are taxed on their worldwide income. However, non-residents are taxed only on their Latvian-sourced income.

4.2.1 Permanent Establishment

[**173**] A permanent establishment (PE) of a Latvian non-resident is considered a separate domestic taxpayer for the purpose of the application of all taxes. A PE of a non-resident must pay taxes in accordance with the laws of the Republic of Latvia on income derived in Latvia, its territorial waters and air space, for income earned abroad but which pertains to this establishment, as well as other taxes in accordance with the provisions of specific tax laws.

[**174**] A non-resident has a PE in Latvia if all of the following conditions are met concurrently:

(1) the non-resident uses a fixed place of business in Latvia;
(2) the place of business is used permanently or has been established for the purpose of being utilized permanently; and
(3) the place of business is used for carrying on business activity.

[**175**] It should also be noted that a non-resident has a PE in Latvia if the non-resident carries on at least one of the following activities in Latvia:

(1) he/she uses a building site or carries out construction, assembly or installation works or performs supervisory or consultative functions related to the building site or the said works;
(2) he/she uses equipment or installations, drilling platforms or special ships intended for the research or extraction of natural resources or carries out supervisory or consultative work related thereto;

(3) within a time period or time periods, which in aggregate exceed thirty days in any six-month period, he/she provides services including consulting, management and technical services, engaging its employees or associated personnel; or
(4) he/she uses the operation of a natural, legal or other person for the benefit of its business activities if the person referred to has authority and habitually exercises (more than once in a taxation period) that authority to conclude contracts in the name of a foreign undertaking.

4.2.2 Main Taxes

Corporate income tax

[176] As of 1 January 2018, Latvian companies and branches/PE of non-residents pay CIT only when distributing profits or incurring expenses unrelated to business activities.

Thus, a taxpayer does not pay tax on annual profit until it distributes dividends, deemed dividends, or deemed profits. The CIT rate is 20%, which is applied to the profit distributed (whose value is divided by a coefficient of 0.8 prior to the application of CIT). Thus, the effective CIT rate is 25%. The taxpayer does not pay CIT in advance.

Profit distribution includes regular and extraordinary dividends. The deemed profit includes the expenses not related to economic activity, the bad debts' write-off, the increased interest payments (thin cap rule), the loan to the related person, transfer pricing adjustments, the liquidation quota, the value of assets transferred abroad, hybrid mismatches, the value of assets transferred to another person in reorganization proceedings, the value of such asset which is transferred by a taxpayer of Latvia to its PE abroad for the performance of economic activity, if as a result of the transfer of the asset, Latvia loses the right to impose tax on the transferred asset.

With respect to the income of non-residents, if the non-resident entity has no PE in Latvia, the particular income of the non-resident would be subject to several withholding taxes (please *see* the section *Structuring the Investment – Withholding Taxes* below).

Taxes on capital gains

Personal income tax (PIT) at the rate of 20% is applicable to capital gains (e.g., on the sale of shares, securities, virtual currency, and real estate) earned by private individuals. Income from capital other than capital gains (e.g., dividend income and interest income) is subject to PIT at the rate of 20%.

Since 2018, companies have been released from the application of CIT to capital gains earned from the sale of shares owned directly if the shares have been held for a period of at least thirty-six months and the closed-ended alternative investment fund if specific conditions are met, except for shares of companies located offshore. In this case, if the recipient of dividends is a private individual, then the company applying the above exemption must withhold PIT at the rate of 20%.

Value added tax (VAT) or sales taxes or other taxes on revenue/sales

Generally, the provision of services and the sale of goods constitute a VAT-taxable transaction. The VAT rates applicable are 21% (the general VAT rate), 5% and 12% (reduced rates applicable to certain types of transactions) and 0% (applicable, e.g., to goods leaving Latvia to the territory of another Member State of the EU).

Stamp duties or other taxes on land transactions

Regarding transactions involving land, stamp duty applies for corroboration of ownership rights:

(a) on the purchase of immovable property: 2% of the purchase price;
(b) on the endowment of immovable property: 3% of the value of the property;
(c) on the purchase or endowment of immovable property to third-degree relatives: 0.5% of the value of the property;
(d) on the investment of immovable property into the share capital of the company: 1% of the investment value;
(e) on the purchase of apartments carried out by a company: 6% of the transaction value.

In the case of corroboration of collateral rights, a stamp duty applies at the rate of 0.1% of the value of the loan or the value of the claim.

There is an exemption to stamp duty in cases where a company obtains immovable property due to reorganization.

Other taxes on land or real estate

Real estate tax (RET) applies to the cadastral value of the immovable property. The RET rate varies from 0.2% up to 3% depending upon the type of the property as well as the owner of the property. The general RET rate applicable to immovable property, which is used in business activities, is 1.5% – opportunities for applying the 0.2–0.6% tax rates are generally reserved for residential buildings, whereas the 3% tax rate is reserved for derelict buildings, which endanger life and health, as well as buildings which have exceeded the maximum construction time.

Taxes imposed on employers

With respect to employment taxes, employers pay the employers' part of social security contributions at a rate of 23.59% of the gross salary of the employee. It is the employer's responsibility to withhold and declare payroll taxes and to transfer them to the state budget.

In addition, the employer pays business risk duty for each employee in an amount of EUR0.36 per month.

Customs and Excise duties

Latvia imposes customs duties on the import or export of goods. The customs policy is defined at the EU level, and the value of the customs duty depends on the type and value of the relevant goods.

Excise duty is applied to several types of goods:

(a) Alcoholic beverages.
(b) Tobacco.
(c) Petroleum production.
(d) Natural gas.
(e) Non-alcoholic beverages and coffee.

The value of the excise duty depends on each particular product, which is subject to excise duties.

4.3 Tax Consolidation Group Relief of Gains and Losses

[177] What scope exists for the use of gains or losses of the target company elsewhere within the purchaser's group?

Losses cannot be transferred from one company of the group to another. Also, the profit (gains) cannot be transferred from one company of the group to another.

Are the profits of a foreign subsidiary imputed to a parent company which is tax-resident in Latvia?

[178] If the foreign subsidiary is an independent entity (daughter company), the profit would not be imputed to the parent company's profit and taxed in Latvia. However, if the foreign subsidiary is a branch or PE, the profit of the subsidiary will also constitute profit of the parent company. In such cases, the provisions of tax treaties on avoidance of double taxation would apply.

4.4 Tax Considerations Arising on M&A Transactions

Individual vendors

[179] The following tax consequences apply:

(1) Tax on capital gains – the difference between the sales value and the original purchase and investment value of the shares will be subject to 20% PIT.
(2) Transfer pricing rules – if a sale of shares is carried out between related parties, the sales value of the shares has to be determined at market rates.

Corporate vendors

[180] The following tax consequences apply:

(1) Exemption from capital gains tax – capital gains due to sale of shares are released from CIT if the directly owned shares sold have been held for at least thirty-six months, except to shares of an offshore company and shares, which carry an immovable property located in Latvia. Finally, the

special exemption regime does not apply if the structure has been set up with the aim of using this regime.

(2) Tax on dividends – dividend distribution is a taxable event. The profit paid out as dividends from the sale of shares to a shareholder – being a private individual – will be subject to 20% PIT. The profit paid out to legal persons as dividends from the sale of shares will not be taxed except if paid to offshore jurisdictions (please see rules for special exemption above).

(3) Transfer pricing rules – if a sale of shares is carried out between related parties, the sales value of the shares has to be determined at market rates.

From the purchaser's perspective – Individual purchaser

[181] Change of ownership at the company level does not affect taxation, except if the change of ownership reduces the amount of fixed capital that was previously formed by capitalizing profits.

Corporate purchaser

[182] Change of ownership at the company level does not affect taxation, except if the change of ownership reduces the amount of fixed capital that was previously formed by capitalizing profits.

Sale of assets (for cash, shares or other securities) From the vendor's perspective – Individual vendor

[183] The following tax consequences apply:

(1) Tax on capital gains – the difference between the sale value and the original purchase and investment value of capital assets will be subject to 20% PIT.

(2) Transfer pricing rules – if a sale of assets is carried out between related parties, the sale value of the assets has to be determined at market rates.

Corporate vendor

[184] The following tax consequences apply:

(1) Tax on capital gains – the difference between the sale value and the purchase value of the assets will be subject to CIT only at the moment of profit distribution unless specific exemptions apply.

(2) Tax on dividends – At the moment of dividend distribution, CIT is applied. The profit paid out to private individuals as dividends from the sale of the shares owed directly or the closed-ended alternative investment fund if the holding period is at least thirty-six months and the other conditions are met will be subject to 20% PIT withholding. The profit paid out to legal persons as dividends from the sale of the above-mentioned shares will not be taxed. The profit paid out to private individuals and/or legal persons as dividends from the sale of the other assets will be subject to CIT.

(3) Transfer pricing rules – if a sale of assets is carried out between related parties, the sale value of the assets must be determined at market rates.
(4) Input VAT corrections – the sale of used real estate might lead to a correction of the input VAT deducted for the past periods.
(5) The results of asset impairment for annual reporting purposes do not affect taxation.

From the purchaser's perspective – Individual purchaser

Stamp duty at the rate of 1.5% is applicable for registration of real estate in the land register.

Corporate purchaser

(1) 3% withholding tax on payments made by resident corporate purchasers to non-residents for purchase of real estate.
(2) 2% stamp duty for registration of real estate in the land register.

To what extent are values negotiable between the parties in any discussion on price? To what extent are they required to be determined by independent assessment?

The value of shares or assets is determined on the basis of negotiations between the seller and purchaser, which, together or separately, can decide to make an independent assessment of the value of shares or assets. The law does not provide such an obligation unless the sale of shares or assets is carried out between related parties.

Are there any tax reliefs, exemptions or deferrals available for particular types of amalgamation or reorganization? Is it possible and/or customary to obtain advance tax clearances from the relevant tax authorities?

To be tax-neutral, the reorganization procedure must comply with the definition and special conditions described in the CIT law; namely, the transfer of assets and creditors is performed in exchange for shares, and the transferred assets continue to be used by CIT payers in Latvia.

There is no specific tax relief available within an amalgamation or reorganization.

Taxpayers are entitled to ask for written opinions or binding rulings from the Latvian tax authorities. The law provides an obligation on the Latvian tax authorities to issue their opinions within a thirty-day period, with additional rights to extend the term if this is needed.

To what extent are unused tax losses in the target company available for use by a foreign-owned acquirer or its subsidiaries? Are there any restrictions on the carry forward of losses? (e.g., on a change of control of the target company?)

Starting in 2018, a company does not have tax losses. Thus, any loss transfer is not possible. A taxpayer may use 15% of the tax losses incurred before 31 December 2017 to reduce the CIT calculated on the dividends in the reporting year (which starts in 2018), but no later than 31 December 2022. Change of ownership at the company level does not affect taxation.

To what extent are deferred payments, retentions, holdbacks and 'earn-outs' commonly used/acceptable as a means of mitigating transaction risks? How are these dealt with from a tax perspective?

Latvian tax laws do not provide separate taxation principles in relation to deferred payments and similar monetary instruments, which are applied for the purposes of mitigation of transaction risks.

Are acquisition expenses generally deductible as business expenses?

Yes, acquisition expenses are generally deductible as regular business costs for tax purposes.

4.5 Structuring the Investment: Withholding Taxes

[185] Are payments to non-residents subject to withholding taxes (i.e., a tax collected at source by the payer)? As regards withholding and other taxes, how are the following taxed?

- *Dividends paid to foreign corporate/group shareholders?*

Dividends are not subject to withholding taxes. Dividends distributed from profits generated as of 2018 are subject to CIT at the effective rate of 25% at the level of payer. Dividends from profits formed before 2017 are not taxable except dividends paid to offshore jurisdictions.

- *Dividends paid to foreign individual shareholders?*

Dividends distributed from profits generated as of 2018 are subject to CIT at the effective rate of 25%. If CIT on dividends has been paid, no PIT is applied. Dividend payments from profits formed before 2017 should be subject to a PIT rate of 20%. However, double tax treaty provisions should be applicable.

- *Dividends received from foreign subsidiaries/affiliates? (Are these exempt from further taxes in your jurisdiction?)*

Dividends received from foreign subsidiaries are non-taxable in Latvia (*pass-through* dividends principle). A taxpayer who meets the statutory conditions may reduce the amount of dividends paid by the amount of dividends received from subsidiaries except for dividends received from offshore jurisdictions.

- *Interest paid to foreign corporate/group shareholders or affiliates?*

Non-taxable, except for interest payments made to offshore jurisdictions.

- *Interest received from foreign corporate/group shareholders or affiliates?*

Interest received is considered regular business income, being subject to tax upon distribution of dividends.

- *Intellectual property (IP) royalties paid to foreign corporate/group shareholders or affiliates?*

Non-taxable, except for IP royalties made to offshore jurisdictions.

- *Intellectual property (IP) royalties received from foreign corporate/group shareholders or affiliates?*

Royalties received are considered regular business income, being subject to tax upon distribution of dividends.

- *Management or consultancy fees paid to foreign corporate/group shareholders or affiliates?*

Withholding tax at the rate of 20% applies to management and consultancy fees paid to non-residents. In most cases, the rate can be reduced to 0% by applying the provisions of double tax treaties.

- *Payments to non-residents in respect of the purchase or renting of immovable property?*

If a non-resident sells an immovable property located in Latvia, a withholding tax at the rate of 3% applies.

If a non-resident gains income from immovable property located in Latvia, a withholding tax at the rate of 5% applies.

Is there a wide network of double tax treaties affecting the payment of withholding taxes?

There are more than fifty double tax treaties which are currently applicable. Several treaties have been signed but have not yet come into effect. Since 16 May 2022, Latvia has terminated the double tax treaty with the Russian Federation.

What are the main requirements for obtaining relief from the obligation to withhold under these treaties?

In order to apply the relief provided by the double tax treaty, a residence certificate should be in place prior to making the relevant payment.

Would you say there are any 'typical' or commonly used investment structures in your jurisdiction to take advantage of these treaties?

The double tax treaties do not provide specific advantageous investment structures.

4.6 Debt Financing

Are finance costs associated with the acquisition generally deductible?

[186] Finance costs which are related to the acquisition are generally deductible for CIT purposes.

4.7 Thin Capitalization

[187] Thin capitalization rules do apply in Latvia. One of the following calculations should be applied:

(1) Taxable income must be increased by interest payments in proportion to the extent to which the average amount of debt obligations in the taxation period (in respect of which the interest payments are calculated) exceeds an amount equal to four times the amount of own capital reflected in the taxpayer's annual accounts, which is reduced by the conversion of long-term deposits into reserves and other reserves, which have not been created as a result of the division of profits.
(2) When the difference between interest payments and interest income in a tax year exceeds EUR3 m, the taxable amount shall include the amount of interest payments exceeding 30% of the profit before CIT shown in the profit or loss account for the tax year, increased by interest payments and depreciation.

[188] If the taxable income has to be increased according to both calculations, the calculation yielding the largest value has to be applied.

[189] The particular provisions are not applicable to credit institutions and insurance companies. Also, these provisions do not apply to interest payments for loans which have been received from a credit institution which is a resident of Latvia or another Member State of the EU or a state of the EEA, or a resident of any state with which Latvia has entered into a convention or agreement for the avoidance of double taxation and non-payment of taxes, if the relevant convention or agreement has come into force, as well as from the Treasury of the Republic of Latvia, the Nordic Investment Bank, the European Bank for Reconstruction and Development, the European Investment Bank, the Council of Europe Development Bank and the World Bank group.

[190] In addition, the second provision referred to above is not applicable to interest payments on loans which have been received from any such financial institution as it complies with the following criteria:

(1) It is a resident of Latvia or another Member State of the EU or a state of the EEA, or a resident of any state with which Latvia has entered into a convention or agreement for the avoidance of double taxation and non-payment of taxes if the relevant convention or agreement has come into force.
(2) It provides credit services or financial leasing services, and the supervision thereof is performed by the supervisory authority of credit institutions or finance of the relevant state.

4.8 Transfer Pricing

[191] Transfer pricing rules apply in Latvia. Namely, the prices charged within transactions between related parties (both local and foreign) have to correspond to arm's-length value.

[192] The tax legislative acts also make it necessary to justify the transfer prices by holding appropriate transfer pricing documentation (as per the OECD guidelines). Depending on the total volume of the taxpayer's intra-group transactions and its net turnover, a three-level approach to transfer pricing documentation is applicable: country-by-country report, master file and local file.

Formally, a taxpayer is not required to prepare or submit to the tax authorities transfer pricing documentation if the total volume of the taxpayer's foreign intra-group transactions does not exceed EUR250 000 per annum. Also, formally, transfer pricing documentation is not required for domestic-related party transactions. However, the requirement for the taxpayer to be able to prove the compliance of its applied transfer prices to intra-group transactions (including with domestic-related companies) with the arm's-length principle is still applicable.

If requested by the tax authorities, the taxpayer must, according to its own discretion, verify and provide information demonstrating that the transfer prices applied to the controlled intra-group transactions are consistent with the arm's-length principle.

[193] **Local file.** The taxpayer is required to, within twelve months after the end of the relevant accounting year, prepare and, if the tax administration so requests, submit to it within one month after receipt of the request local file if the total volume of the controlled intra-group transactions exceeds EUR250 000 for the relevant accounting year, but does not exceed EUR5 m.

Master file. The taxpayer is required to, within twelve months after the end of the relevant accounting year, prepare and, if the tax administration so requests, submit to it within one month after receipt of the request a master file if the net turnover of the taxpayer in the relevant accounting year does not exceed EUR50 m and the total volume of the controlled intra-group transactions does not exceed EUR15 m in the relevant accounting year, but exceeds EUR5 m.

Penalties for late submission and non-compliance with the requirements for preparation of transfer pricing documentation at the amount of 1% of the controlled transaction amount but not exceeding EUR100 000.

Currently, transfer pricing audits are one of the most common reviews performed by the tax authorities, as the necessity of having proper supporting documentation was implemented as of 1 January 2013. The tax authorities do challenge the prices applied in cases where there is no transfer pricing documentation in place. However, if the company holds valid transfer pricing documentation, the risk that the transfer prices will be challenged tends to be rather low.

5 EMPLOYMENT CONSIDERATIONS

5.1 Legislative Framework

[194] The main legislative framework affecting labour and employment in Latvia is the *Labour Law*.

[195] The *Labour Law* prescribes that the rights and duties of the transferor of an undertaking that arise from employment relationships applicable at the moment of transfer of the undertaking must devolve to the acquirer of the undertaking. The transfer of an undertaking may not of itself form the basis for notice of termination of an employment contract. Such provision does not restrict the right of an employer to give notice of termination of an employment contract if such notice is based on the performance of economic, organizational, technological, or similar measures in the undertaking.

[196] The board of a company does not have an obligation to consult with its employees, and it cannot block any company's transactions. However, both the transferor of an undertaking and the acquirer of an undertaking have a duty to inform their employees or their representatives regarding the date of transfer of the undertaking or the expected date of transfer; the reasons for the transfer of the undertaking; the legal, economic, and social consequences of the transfer; as well as of the measures which will be taken with respect to employees.

[197] The role and influence of employee work councils in Latvia, compared with other European countries, tend to be weak. However, work councils, when performing their duties, have the right to receive information (the employer transfers information to employee representatives, allowing them to become acquainted with the relevant issue and to investigate it) on a timely basis and to consult (exchange views and engage in dialogue with the employer for the purpose of achieving agreement) with the employer before the employer takes any decisions which may affect the interests of employees, in particular decisions which may substantially affect work remuneration, working conditions and employment in the undertaking.

[198] In all cases whether for 'blue-collar workers' or 'white-collar workers', an employer has the right to give a written notice of termination of an employment contract only on the basis of circumstances related to the conduct of the employee, his or her abilities or of economic, organizational, technological measures or measures of a similar nature in the undertaking.

[199] The *Labour Law* contains a number of special protections for certain categories of employees. An employer is prohibited from giving a notice of termination of an employment contract to a pregnant woman, a woman during the period of one year after the birth of a child, a breastfeeding woman during the whole period of breastfeeding (but until no later than the child reaching an age of 2 years) and an employee who is declared to be a disabled person. Also, an employer does not have the right to give notice of termination to an employee during a period of temporary incapacity of such employee.

[200] An employer is prohibited from giving notice of termination of an employment contract to an employee who is a member of a trade union without the prior consent of the relevant trade union in most cases. It should be noted that with the exception of the public sector (such as healthcare and police) and areas of major state monopolies (e.g., energy and railroads), which have strongly established relations between employers and capable trade unions, Latvian trade unions are not considered particularly effective.

[201] When giving notice of termination of an employment contract in the cases set out in the law, an employer has a duty to observe the mandatory notice period (generally one month, but less in the event of termination due to serious misconduct by the employee – even immediate, e.g., in the event of an employee being under the influence of drugs or alcohol during work) and to pay applicable severance pay, expressed as a multiple of the employee's average monthly earnings and tied to the total period of employment. Severance pay does not have to be paid if the employee is terminated for substantial violations of the labour agreement, law or work safety, such as intoxication, as mentioned above. The collective bargaining process in Latvia is in its infancy and can fairly be described as weak.

5.2 Retention of Key Management and Employees

[202] It is not uncommon to include, in transfer documentation, provisions for the retention of key management and employees.

[203] The main steps available to purchasers to ensure the continuation of individual vendors, members of the management team or other key employees are to negotiate separate contracts with them. Theoretically, this could be backed up by retention of the proceeds of sale if the vendor so agrees.

[204] Employment agreements may contain non-competition clauses but are limited in time (no more than two years) and scope. They may only restrict the former employee from future employment in a position similar to the existing one and may not restrict future employment in the employer's area of commercial activity, regardless of position. Such non-competition clauses give rise to an ongoing obligation to pay a premium for the observance of such provisions, which must be consistent with the restriction. A figure of 50% of average monthly earnings has been cited as a guideline in court practice. Failure to observe the above restrictions will render the non-competition clause unenforceable. Non-competition with vendors is a matter of contract.

5.3 Treatment of Foreign Employees

[205] There are no special restrictions affecting foreign managers and directors. The legislation prescribes that an employee coming from a country which is not a Member State of the EU, the European Economic Area or the Swiss Confederation has to have a work and residence permit and, if necessary, also a visa.

[206] An employer who posts an employee to perform work in Latvia has a duty, prior to posting the employee, to inform the State Labour Inspectorate in writing regarding such posted employee, providing a certification that the posted employee who is a third-country national legally works for an employer in the EU Member State, the European Economic Area or the Swiss Confederation.

[207] Generally, it takes one to three months to receive work and residence permits, and it costs approximately EUR285–EUR430.

[208] Latvian tax residents are taxed on their worldwide income. However, foreign tax residents (i.e., Latvian non-residents for tax purposes) are taxed only on their Latvian-sourced income. The Law on PIT provides a list of types of non-resident income which are taxable in Latvia (e.g., income from professional activities performed in Latvia or for the benefit of a Latvian company and income from the sale of real estate located in Latvia).

[209] The residency determination criteria are provided in the Law on Taxes and Fees, which provides that for the purpose of the tax law, a natural person should be considered a resident of Latvia if:

(1) the registered place of residence of such person is the Republic of Latvia; or
(2) such person stays in the Republic of Latvia for 183 days or longer during any twelve-month period beginning or ending in a tax year; or
(3) such person is a Latvian citizen who is employed in a foreign country by the government of the Republic of Latvia.

[210] As Latvia has concluded a number of treaties on avoidance of double taxation of income, the criteria for the determination of residence provided for in those treaties are also applicable.

After 24 February 2022, the Latvian parliament amended related immigration regulations in order to ease the entrance of Ukrainian nationals into Latvia and facilitate their further employment.

5.3.1 Income Tax, Social Security Contributions

[211] Within employment relationships, the following taxes are applicable:

(1) On 1 January 2018, progressive PIT rates were introduced as follows: 20% for income not exceeding EUR20 004 per year; 23% for income between EUR20 004 and EUR78 100 per year; and 31% for income exceeding EUR78 100 per year.

The tax on annual income of more than EUR62 800 per year will be calculated in a recapitulative order when submitting the annual income declaration. If a payroll tax book is not submitted at a place of employment, the salary tax rate will be 23% regardless of monthly income.

(2) Mandatory social security contributions are payable at the rate of 34.09% (employee's liability, 10.5% and employer's liability, 23.59%). Slightly

lower tax rates are applicable to specific types of employees (e.g., pensioners and disabled persons). The taxable object is all employment-related income. In 2022, the maximum income subject to mandatory social security contributions was EUR78 100 (the excess of income over this level is not subject to mandatory social security contributions). In 2016, a new related tax was adopted called the solidarity tax. This tax applies to the same types of income and has the same rates as social contributions but is applicable to that part of yearly income above EUR78 100. While there are some differences about the sub-budgets to which proceeds from this tax are transferred, the introduction of the solidarity tax effectively abolished the above maximum limit on social contributions.

(3) Business risk duty is levied in the amount of EUR0.36 per employee per month.

5.3.2 Directors' Liability

[212] Exposure to liability is an issue for directors, despite the increasing availability of directors' liability insurance. The standard to which directors are held is that of a prudent manager. Any derogation from such standard can theoretically trigger personal liability. It is common to discharge directors from their liability for the past accounting year upon adoption of the annual report, assuming the shareholders or supervisory council has not found their performance lacking.

[213] The liability of directors is not limited to civil liability – in the event of the director's actions substantially harming the interests of the state or another person, a number of violations can go from civil liability or administrative fines to criminal liability, such as for competition and tax violations. Criteria for determining if harm is substantial are set out in the Law of Entry into Force and Application of the Criminal Law of Latvia and are generally tied to multiples of the minimum wage (5–10 depending on circumstances and other harm inflicted) and can be considered a relatively low threshold.

6 ACCOUNTING TREATMENT

The format and content of group accounts

[214] The format and content of group accounts are set out in the 2016 *Law on Annual Reports and Consolidated Annual Reports*. The law regulates when consolidated accounts need to be prepared and when the financial statements are audited by a sworn auditor. Companies are classified as micro, small, medium or large depending on their accounts, yearly turnover and number of employees, and the contents required of annual reports differ for each category. Groups of companies are similarly classified.

International Financial Reporting Standards (IFRS) implementation

IFRS is mandatory for financial institutions such as banks and investment brokerage companies. IFRS is mandatory for listed companies whose securities are included *in the official list.*

IFRS is mandatory for all listed companies that prepare consolidated accounts.

IFRS is not mandatory for other companies. However, they are allowed to apply IFRS for consolidated accounts.

Are companies at liberty to adopt merger accounting as well as acquisition accounting?

This particular issue is not specifically defined under the local law. Accordingly, the IFRS treatment is applied to such cases.

Are fair values affected by any changes in the assets or liabilities that result from the intentions of the acquirer or from events occurring after the acquisition, or should such changes be dealt with as post-acquisition items?

These particular issues are not specifically defined under the local law. Accordingly, the IFRS treatment is applied to such cases.

What scope is there for 'provisioning'? How are the costs of any proposed reorganization and/or integration of the acquired business dealt with?

These particular issues are not specifically defined under the local law. Accordingly, the IFRS treatment is applied to such cases.

If companies are required to capitalize goodwill, are they required to amortize it through the P&L account, and if so, over what period are they required to do this?

No, the goodwill is tested for impairment annually.

Can the life of acquired goodwill (or goodwill arising on consolidation) be regarded as 'indefinite' and therefore not subject to amortization?

Yes, the acquired goodwill can be treated as 'indefinite'.

Is it mandatory to undertake impairment reviews? If so, how often?

It is necessary to undertake impairment reviews on an annual basis.

When/under what circumstances/are intangible assets recognized?

The difference arising as a result of mutual exclusion (procedure performed within equity consolidation) is attributed to the value of the consolidated balance sheet item by increasing or reducing it according to whether the value of these items is greater or less than the value initially indicated in the balance sheet of the subsidiary company included in the consolidation. If the difference referred to cannot be attributed fully to the items of the consolidated balance sheet, any remaining positive amount should be indicated in a separate item, 'Goodwill', on the asset side of the balance sheet. The remaining negative difference should be immediately included in the profit or loss account.

Only rights acquired in exchange for valuable consideration may be set out in the investments in the intangible assets item: 'Concessions, Patents, Licenses,

Trade Marks and Similar Rights'. Research costs and start-up expenditures may not be capitalized. Development costs may be included in the balance sheet in the intangible investment item 'Development Costs' only if certain criteria are met.

Are intangible assets amortized over their useful lives, or are they subject to impairment reviews? If the latter, how often?

The amortization treatment depends on the assets concerned. Usually, intangibles (such as goodwill, trademarks and similar) are subject to impairment reviews.

The amount indicated under the consolidated balance sheet item 'Goodwill', after the initial accounting, should be valued as costs, from which accumulated losses from the reduction in value should be deducted. The parent company of the group of companies, for the purposes of preparation of consolidated financial statements at the end of each accounting year, should evaluate whether the balance sheet value of the amount indicated under the consolidated balance sheet item 'Goodwill' has or has not reduced.

Is negative goodwill recognized as a balance sheet item, or is it credited to the profit and loss account?

Negative goodwill is recognized as income in the profit/loss account.

Are acquisition costs expensed in the period in which they are incurred, or are they capitalized?

The acquisition costs are capitalized.

What is the effective date of acquisition from which profits of the target company(ies) are brought into the acquiring company's P&L account? How/where is this defined?

Revenue and costs of a subsidiary undertaking of the group of companies are included in the consolidated profit or loss account with effect from the date on which such undertaking has become a subsidiary undertaking of the group of companies and until the date on which the control of the parent undertaking of the group of companies over such subsidiary undertaking ends.

How are deferred and/or contingent consideration payments valued? (And do any changes in such values affect the P&L account, or do they result in adjustments to the goodwill figure?)

These particular questions are not specifically defined under the local law. Accordingly, the IFRS treatment is applied to such cases.

From the perspective of the vendor, when can any profit arising from the sale be brought into its P&L account? Are there differences between 'extraordinary items' and 'exceptional items' which will determine whether such profits appear 'above the line' or 'below the line'?

These particular questions are not specifically defined under the local law. Accordingly, the IFRS treatment is applied to such cases.

7 FUTURE DEVELOPMENTS

[215] Recent geopolitics events have impacted all EU countries, including Latvia. Until 24 February 2022, many Latvian businesses had connections with Russia and Belarus, and after the beginning of the war, many Latvian companies and businesses had to restructure their commercial activity. A number of Russian and Belarusian businesses migrated into Latvia, and some western investors relocated their business places into Latvia, for example, in the IT sector.

Compliance issues regarding AML requirements figure prominently in the business landscape.

www.ingramcontent.com/pod-product-compliance
Lightning Source LLC
Chambersburg PA
CBHW072244240926
51846CB00012B/611